New Rules of Marriage

*How It Can Help You Keep Love
for the Married and the Coupled Up*

DAVID BOBKER

CONTENTS

FOREWORD

Connecting with someone romantically, emotionally, and physically can be really amazing. However, there is a lot of work that goes into building a good relationship.

Women have changed in the past twenty-five years. They have become strong, independent, confident and happy. However, many men remain irresponsible and emotionless.

Falling in love is great, but what about your happiness ever after? In order to go the distance with your significant other, it is crucial to ask the question: *What makes a relationship work?*

"The New Rules of Marriage" will introduce you to a whole new kind of relationship, based on the idea that women are capable of transforming their marriage, while men give the right support.

The book also gives theory, assumption and examples from which express meaningful lessons for yourself and your great and lovely family. Roles of each factor and other infinitesimal moment in love are recorded through per page of "The New Rules of Marriage".

MARRIAGE

Meaning

When someone begins on that arrangement called marriage, he is getting into something which is, to say the least, adventurous. When a couple get married, they are doing something they know nothing about. And, from all indications, when they have tried it more than once, they know no more about it the second time than they did the first.

Marriage is the foundation of the family unit. In this society and time, the family is the closest knit, self-perpetuating, self-protecting unit. It is necessary economically and otherwise to the society the way it is set up in present time. A culture will go by the boards if its basic building block, the family, is removed as a valid building block. So one can be fairly sure that he who destroys marriage destroys the civilization.

The marriage relationship, basically, is a *postulated* relationship. A *postulate* is a conclusion, decision or resolution about something. When people stop postulating a marriage, it ceases to exist. That is what happens to most marriages. It isn't the other way around. It isn't that all men are evil, so therefore, contracts such as marriage dissolve usually in infidelity and go all to pieces. That is not true. The reverse is true. When you have a purely postulated relationship, you have to continue to create it. And a family which doesn't continue to create itself as a family will cease to exist as a family. That's about all you need to know about it.

Where people are having trouble with marriage, it is because they are expecting it to run on automatic. They think it will hang together through no effort of their own; unfortunately, it won't. It has to be created.

Perhaps someone whose parents weren't making too good a go of it, looked at this and decided, "Now, look at that! This institution which is inherent in nature, which nothing will ever change, doesn't perpetuate itself and is not much good because it isn't hanging together."

He had a failure. He probably tried to postulate the family into a unit when he was very young. He was working at it, trying to get a Papa - love - Mama thing going one way or the other, trying to show them that they had something to live for and so forth.

As a matter of fact, one of the reasons a child gets himself injured is to make his parents realize they have responsibilities for the family. Childhood illness and all this sort of thing occur directly after familial upsets.

Nonetheless, whether an individual had in his own parents a good example of a stable marriage or not, it has nothing to do with whether or not he can make a successful marriage.

If you think that everything else is rigged to perpetuate a marriage while you're not trying to keep it going, of course it will end up in destruction. But if you approach this with the realization that a marriage is something you have to postulate into existence and keep there, and when you stop working at it, it will cease, and if you know the technology contained in the remaining part of this course, you can make any marriage stick or you can recover any facet of any marriage, or plaster one back together again any way you want to. But it takes a little doing and it takes a little guts and that is an understatement.

Purpose

Marriage is the intimate union and equal partnership of a man and a woman. It comes to us from the hand of God, who created male and female in his image, so that they might become one body and might be fertile and multiply (See Genesis chapters 1 and 2). Though man and woman are equal as God's children, they are created with important differences that allow them to give themselves and to receive the other as a gift.

Marriage is both a natural institution and a sacred union because it is rooted in the divine plan of creation. In addition, the Catholic Church teaches that the valid marriage between two baptized Christians is also a sacrament – a saving reality and a symbol of Christ's love for his church (See Ephesians 5:25-33). In every marriage the spouses make a contract with each other. In a sacramental marriage the couple also enters into a covenant in which their love is sealed and strengthened by God's love.

The free consent of the spouses makes a marriage. From this consent and from the sexual consummation of marriage a special bond arises between husband and wife. This bond is lifelong and exclusive. The marriage bond has been established by God and so it cannot be dissolved.

In the Latin Rite of the Catholic Church, the priest or deacon, the two official witnesses, and the congregation all witness the exchange of consent by the couple who themselves are considered to be the ministers of the sacrament. In the Eastern Churches the sacrament is conferred by the priest's blessing after receiving the couple's consent.

Permanency, exclusivity, and faithfulness are essential to marriage because they foster and protect the two equal purposes of marriage. These two purposes are growth in mutual love between the spouses (unitive) and the generation and education of children (procreative).

The mutual love of a married couple should always be open to new life. This openness is expressed powerfully in the sexual union of husband and wife. The power to create a child with God is at the heart of what spouses share with each other in sexual intercourse. Mutual love includes the mutual gift of fertility. Couples who are not able to conceive or who are beyond their child-bearing years can still express openness to life. They can share their generative love with grandchildren, other children and families, and the wider community.

As a result of their baptism, all Christians are called to a life of holiness. This divine calling, or vocation, can be lived in marriage, or in the single life, or in the priesthood or consecrated (religious) life. No one vocation is superior to or inferior to another. Each one involves a specific kind of commitment that flows from one's gifts and is further strengthened by God's grace. All vocations make a unique contribution to the life and mission of the Church.

The family arises from marriage. Parents, children, and family members form what is called a domestic church or church of the home. This is the primary unit of the Church – the place where the Church lives in the daily love, care, hospitality, sacrifice, forgiveness, prayer and faith of ordinary families.

MAKE LOVE WORKS

Relationship

What are some tips for having a great relationship?

No relationship is perfect all the time. But in a healthy relationship, both people feel good about the relationship most of the time. A great relationship takes more than attraction — it takes work, and both of you have to be willing to put in the effort. Here are some tips for building a healthy relationship:

Love yourself. Being comfortable with who you are means you'll be a happier partner.

Communicate. Talk to your partner about your feelings. Ask questions and listen to their answers. If you're upset, say so — don't make your partner try to figure out what's up. Talking through problems builds trust and makes your relationship stronger. And it's not all about how to deal with your problems — don't forget to let them know when something they do makes you happy.

Be honest. Be truthful with each other about what you do, think, and feel. Honesty creates trust. Few things harm a relationship more than lies.

Give each other some space. Couple's time is great, but spending all your time together isn't. It's healthy to have your own friends and interests outside of the relationship.

Agree to disagree. You're not always going to see eye to eye, and that's OK. The important thing is to respect each other's opinions and ideas.

Forgive and ask for forgiveness. Everybody makes mistakes. Be willing to apologize for yours — and accept your partner's apologies.

Support each other. When your partner does something great, tell them! Your partner should do the same for you.

Talk about sex…openly and honestly. Telling your partner what feels good and what you like and don't like helps you have better sex. Never pressure your partner into doing something they don't want to do, or let your partner pressure you — consent is a must.

Take care of your sexual health. Talk to your partner about how you're going to protect each other against STDs and unintended pregnancy. Practice safer sex and get tested for STDs.

How do I know if my relationship is healthy?

It's good to check in with yourself from time to time to see how you're feeling about your relationship. The questions below focus on romantic and sexual relationships, but they can apply to other kinds of relationships, too. After you've asked yourself these questions, it could be helpful to answer them again from your partner's perspective.

Does your partner listen to and respect your ideas?
Does your partner give you space to spend time with your friends and family?
Do you have fun spending time together?
Do you feel comfortable telling your partner when something they do upsets you?
Do you feel comfortable sharing your thoughts and feelings?
Can you tell your partner what you like sexually?
Does your partner make an effort to get along with your friends and family?
Is your partner proud of your accomplishments and successes?
Does your partner respect your differences?
Can you talk to your partner about birth control and/or safer sex?

Relationships can be complicated, but if you answered "yes" to all of these questions, there's a good chance you're in a healthy relationship. If you answered "no" to two or more questions, you might be in an unhealthy relationship.

How can I make my relationship better?

Keeping your relationship in great shape definitely takes work. Talk to your partner about things that you think could be better. Be clear about what's bothering you, and be respectful. Good communication is a big part of solving problems. If you have trouble working through things on your own, you might consider getting help from someone outside your relationship. Sometimes talking with a counselor or therapist can help couples work through issues and improve their relationships.

You deserve to feel safe in your relationship. Emotional, verbal, or physical abuse is not your fault. Here's how to recognize the signs of an unhealthy relationship and get help.

Unhealthy Relationship

How do I know if my relationship is unhealthy?

Sure, nobody's relationship is perfect, and people make mistakes. But if you feel like you're being treated badly, you probably are. Listen to your gut. Healthy relationships make you feel good about yourself — unhealthy relationships don't.

Lying, cheating, jealousy, and disrespect are signs of an unhealthy relationship. So is trying to control a partner. That includes:

keeping track of where they are and who they hang out with

checking their phone or e-mail without permission

keeping them away from friends or family

telling them they can't do certain activities

preventing them from having money

What are the signs of an abusive relationship?

Anyone can find themselves in an abusive relationship, no matter their age, gender, or sexual orientation. Movies and TV shows that depict abuse might give you the impression that an abusive relationship is only when someone is getting hit or physically hurt. But there are different types of abuse that can affect your body, your emotions, and your self-esteem.

Physical abuse means hitting, kicking, pushing, or hurting someone in any way.

Sexual abuse is forcing your partner to do anything sexual, from kissing to having sex. When you don't consent to sexual activity, it's considered sexual assault or rape, whether you're in a relationship or not.

Verbal abuse is name-calling, put-downs, and using words to hurt someone. **Emotional abuse** is when your partner tries to make you feel bad about yourself. That can mean hurting your feelings on purpose, jealousy, blaming you for the abuse, cheating, or continually criticizing you. Emotional abuse affects your self-esteem.

Reproductive control is pressuring your partner to get pregnant, end a pregnancy, lying about birth control, or other controlling decisions about pregnancy and parenting.

Threats and intimidation use the threat of violence or abuse to control a partner. Threatening children, suicide, or physical violence are all ways to control your behavior.

Isolation is controlling who you see, what you do, and limiting your access to friends, family, and other forms of emotional and financial support.

Each relationship is different, and the signs of an abusive relationship can vary. But all of these behaviors are ways that one person tries to maintain all of the power in a relationship and control their partner.

Sometimes abusive behaviors begin slowly and get worse as time goes on. If you've been feeling devalued, afraid, or controlled, get help. Everyone deserves to be in a relationship where both people feel safe and are respected, trusted, and loved.

How do I get out of an abusive relationship?

If you're in an abusive relationship, know that you're not alone and you deserve better. If your partner hurts you physically, emotionally, or sexually, remember: nothing you said or did justifies their behavior. Everyone gets mad sometimes, but talking things through is the way to deal with problems — not hurting you or putting you down.

Abuse doesn't happen because you did something wrong, or weren't good enough to prevent it from happening. Domestic abuse happens because someone made a choice to manipulate and control you to make themselves more powerful. Remember, you deserve healthy, happy relationships. Abuse of any kind is never OK.

When you break up with an abusive partner, it's important to have a safety plan if you're afraid they might hurt you, your children, or other people you love. Call the National Domestic Violence Hotline to get support and advice and check out their safety plan. If you feel like you're in immediate danger, get away from your partner and call police.

How can I help someone who's in an abusive relationship?

Leaving an unhealthy relationship can be really hard and can take a long time. In fact, it takes an average of 7 tries before someone leaves an abusive partner for good. So don't give up on your loved one if they're not ready to leave or they keep going back. The best thing you can do is listen, be supportive, and when you get the chance, talk about how much better life could be.

Here are more tips:

Be supportive and listen patiently. Having you there and getting support can make a big difference.

Help your loved one recognize that abuse is not "normal" and they don't deserve it.

If your loved one is open to leaving the relationship, develop a safety plan together and identify resources that can help.

Sexual and Reproductive Control

Pressuring someone to have sex or messing with their birth control to cause a pregnancy is called sexual and reproductive coercion. It's a form of abuse.

What should I do if my partner pressures me for sex?

You always have the right to say no to sex. Sexual control is pressuring a partner to do things they don't want to do sexually. It can happen to anyone of any gender or sexual orientation.

Here are some examples of sexual control in relationships:

Trying to get your partner to do something they don't want to do sexually threatening to break up with someone if they don't have sex with you having sex with someone who is too drunk to high to consent to having sex forcing someone to have sex

Some people think if they're in love, or if they're married, they can't say no to sex. But that's not true. No matter what kind of relationship you're in, if you're forced to have sex, it's rape. If you're forced to do something else sexually, it's sexual assault.

You don't deserve to be treated this way. Read more about abusive relationships and how to end them safely.

What if my partner is pressuring me to get pregnant?

Pressuring a partner to get pregnant or messing with birth control to cause a pregnancy is called reproductive control. It's never OK.

Everyone should be able to decide if and when they get pregnant, cause a pregnancy, and have children — without pressure or being manipulated by a partner.

Here are some examples of reproductive control:

Refusing to wear a condom, or pressuring your partner not to use one

Hiding or throwing out birth control

Taking off or breaking condoms to try to cause a pregnancy

Lying about using birth control

Threatening a partner who doesn't want to get pregnant

Forcing a partner to have an abortion or carry a pregnancy to term

If any of these things happen to you, understand that you deserve better.

End a Relationship

What's the best way to break up with someone?

Relationships end for a lot of reasons. Maybe you're not happy with your partner, or maybe you just don't want to be in a relationship right now. Whatever the reason, breaking up can be tough. These tips may help:

Prepare. Think about what you're going to say in advance. You may even want to practice on a friend or in front of a mirror, or write out your thoughts.

Pick the right spot. Talk to your partner somewhere that's comfortable for both of you. If you're worried about safety, somewhere public might be the best choice.

Say it in person. If you feel safe, talk to your partner face to face. E-mailing, texting, or talking on the phone may sound easier, but it's usually not the best option. And don't ask a friend to deliver the news for you.

Be respectful. If your partner asks you why you're breaking up with them, be honest — it could help them have better relationships in the future. But don't insult them or try to hurt them.

Make a clean break. If you really want to be friends, that's fine. But if you're just saying "let's be friends" to let your partner down easier … don't. It can lead to more hurt feelings. Even if you plan to stay friends, give your partner some space. It may help to take a break from seeing or talking to each other for a while.

Stick with your decision. If you feel like you're doing the right thing, don't let your partner try to convince you to stay together. It's normal for someone to cry or get upset during a breakup, and that can be really hard to deal with. But feeling bad or guilty isn't a reason to stay in a relationship.

How can I get over a breakup?

No matter how old you are or how many relationships you've been in, getting over a breakup can be really hard. Let yourself be sad, angry, and hurt. Cry, listen to sad music, go for a run, write in your journal — whatever helps you get your feelings out.

Friends or family can be a great support system, and talking it out may make you feel a lot better. If nothing seems to help and you're feeling depressed, you may want to see a counselor — you can get a referral to one from your local Planned Parenthood health center.

A few more tips:

Don't feel like you have to stay friends. It may seem like a way to keep your ex in your life, but it can be really hard to scale a relationship back to a friendship — especially at first. Same goes for being "friends with benefits." Making a clean break may be hard to do, but it can help you focus on moving forward. Resist the urge to post bad things about your ex on Facebook or other social media — it can lead to a lot of embarrassment and regret. Finally, try not to feel bad about yourself. Your relationship didn't work out, but that doesn't mean there's anything wrong with you — or that you'll never find love again.

Successful Relationship

Falling in love is great, but what about your happily ever after? In order to go the distance with your significant other, it's crucial to ask the question: What makes a relationship work? Because to be perfectly honest, the things that may be catalysts at the beginning of your journey (physical attraction, small talk, similar interests) nine times out of 10 are not the things that keep you together long-term. A truly loving relationship requires many things, one of which is a great partnership.

This requires selflessness, putting someone else first, which is just one surefire sign of a healthy pair. But the truth of the matter is that a relationship is hard work, and you can always find ways to improve your connection. "Relationships that work are the ones that are worked on," says Barton Goldsmith, Ph.D., a psychotherapist and emotional fitness expert. So if you aren't well-versed in all of these key areas, all you might need is to exert a bit of effort. Below, we've rounded up the six signs that you're in a successful relationship.

1. You're Always Honest

Life's tough, and one perk of being part of a pair is that you don't have to do it alone. "Having a partner you can trust creates a buffer between you and the difficulties of the world," says Goldsmith. You need someone you can tell your deepest, darkest secrets to. You also should feel like you can be open and upfront with that person too, no matter how difficult the topic or situation may be. And the feeling should go both ways.

2. You Communicate Well

We've already touched on some common communication problems in relationships (you don't ask interesting questions, you're not really listening, etc.). Psychotherapist and author Deborah Sandella, Ph.D., RN, has told us it's all about tapping into your S.O.'s emotions and having you both feel like you're understood. "In the end, we want to be seen and heard," says Sandella. The good news is only one person needs to be an expert communicator in the relationship—so you can take matters into your own hands.

3. You Have Your Own Lives

Some of the most successful relationships I've seen involve two people who are happy in their own lives and even happier when they're together. By having fulfilling jobs, friends, and passions, and pursuing them alone, you still have a significant sense of self. When you don't have your own activities and revolve your life around your partner, you'll put too much pressure on them and your relationship. "Interdependence means having time to yourself as well as time together," says Goldsmith. "The key is finding the right balance." With a little bit of trial and error, we guarantee you'll find it.

4. You Have Similar Life Goals

If you want to live on different coasts, can't agree on having children, and prioritize opposite things, it probably won't work out. "You both know what you want out of life, what your common goals are, what you wish to accomplish in life, and are firmly committed to achieving these together," says Abigail Brenner, MD, a board-certified psychiatrist, about couples who are successful. As a personal anecdote, I had one friend who couldn't make it work with her long-term boyfriend because he wanted different things and wasn't upfront about it from the beginning.

As soon as she met the right guy who prioritized staying close by their families, buying a house, and traveling (the same goals as hers), she knew she had found her husband.

5. You Spend Quality Time Together

The couple that spends real time together has the ability to improve their connection on a deeper level (and we're not talking about laying on the couch while on your phones). "Engaging in leisure activities with a partner is theorized to increase communication, define roles, and increase marital satisfaction when leisure satisfaction is high or when partners are positive and have strong social skills," one study found. And when you enjoy spending time together, you want to be around that person even more (a surefire sign you're with the right person).

6. You Stay Positive

Life has this ability to throw a wrench into your plans every once in a while, so positivity is key. "You can control your behaviors and even your moods when necessary, and having a loving partner who is willing to be there for you, even when you are struggling, can't help but make your relationship more positive," says Goldsmith. It's all about helping the other person look on the bright side of things when it's hard to see the light at the end of the tunnel. And if that's not love, we're not sure what is.

Now that you know what makes a relationship work, you can evaluate these qualities with your partner and decide which areas might need a little bit more attention. And have fun with it—it shouldn't be a chore.

ROLES OF WOMEN IN MARRIAGE

It is precisely because we want the family to work as a place for real intimacy and long-term commitment which is unequivocally committed to the full equality of power for women in family life, and to full respect for the rights of children. It is important to understand that the patriarchal family structure that predominated in the nineteenth century does not function any longer, and that attempts to re-create it inevitably backfire and undermine family life. Women will continue to leave family situations that are oppressive to them: this is a development that cannot and should not be stopped. So if we want to preserve two-parent families, we must ensure that these families provide an equality of respect, power, and financial opportunity and responsibility that are the only stable bases upon which long-term intimacy can be based.

In this way, we must understand that the movement for equality of power and respect for women represents a force for strengthening family life by creating women who will insist on the kinds of relationships that have real potential for genuine love and intimacy. The breakdown of family life through much of the twentieth century in the United States was often based on the following pattern: women being forced into subordinate and un-respected roles in the family and slowly building up resentment and anger until the stress of the situation broke through, either in the form of behaviors that are labeled "hysteria," "depression" or "psychosis," or in resentful actions that are called "bitchy" or "self-centered," or in leaving the family and seeking divorce. It would be not only morally incorrect but also practically unworkable to try to save the family by convincing women to accept this subordination. If two-parent families are to work, they will do so because this destructive dynamic has been removed and because women have gained real equality of power and respect, at work and at home.

However, it is important to emphasize that it is not in the name of unrestricted individual rights that we make this argument. Rather, it is because we share with many people on all shades of the political spectrum the fundamental belief that a truly human vision is one that is based on the mutual inter-connectedness, dependency, and love between people that we then proceed to argue for those changes that could make these loving relationships possible.

It is for the same reason that we insist that children be treated with respect in families—not out of a commitment to individual rights as the highest value, but out of an understanding that truly loving relationships cannot be compelled and rarely emerge out of force or power plays. It is precisely when children feel most respected that they are most able to give the kind of energy and enthusiasm to their families that make families work best. We do not mean to imply here that equality of respect requires equal power in decisions for children. What it does require is that when limits and restrictions are placed on children they are explained in ways that are appropriate to the developmental level of the child. It also requires the opportunity for children to express their feelings, including negative ones, about the situations they are facing in their family life.

Anyone who has raised children knows how difficult this is. Children quickly learn the "I have rights" rhetoric of the larger society and can use that to resist even valuable instruction that parents have to offer. So it is important to have a community of people who share your values so that parents in any given family are not seen as being merely arbitrary power-mongers when they impose limits on their children. This is increasingly important as television, I-phones, the internet and texting overwhelm parents and shape children into the values of the marketplace way earlier than used to happen in previous historical periods. Here is one of the critical arenas in which parents need to create a counter-culture that resists the pressures of the marketplace as they get communicated by the increasingly prevalent pressures imposed on families by the individualizing impact of the new technologies. These new technologies are not value-neutral—they have a powerful shaping impact precisely because they are perceived as private arenas for children that take them outside family life—for example, by texting during dinner, family trips, family entertainment or family discussions of important shared concerns. So we need to support parents to put limits on the use of these technologies.

One important step is to re-establish the family meals as "time outs" from any use of technologies and instead a sacred time for family interactions without outside distractions. While we support these strategies for parents to provide a nurturing environment for children, we do not believe they should be legislated but we do hope that these approaches to family life will be promoted by government, corporations, social and religious institutions and the like.

Prevalent theoretical approaches

In the literature addressing reconciliation of work and family life, "blurring boundaries" is a frequently applied concept (Gottschall & Vob, 2003). It is closely linked to de-traditionalizing gender relations, that is, the changing meaning of paid work and its spilling over to private life. This may further challenge gender relations, especially as increasingly uncertain occupational biographies for men (Oppenheimer, 1997), seen in more precarious forms of employment and in a decline of the male breadwinner's hip (Cranford, Vosko & Zukewich, 2003), may force more women to become breadwinners (Crompton, 1999; Maetzke & Ostner, 2010). This in turn challenges traditional distributions of power and money in intimate relationships (see Wimbauer, 2003; Ruiner, Hirseland & Schneider, 2011; Lennon, Stewart & Ledermann, 2012).

Increasing maternal employment also challenges the gendered division of childcare. Although one would expect that increases in mothers' employment lead to a more equal sharing of childcare responsibilities between mothers and fathers (Bergmann, 2005), mothers still spend much more time on these tasks than fathers do (Bianchi & Milkie, 2010; Sayer & Gornick, 2011), even though in recent decades, fathers have become involved in care activities more than ever before (Bianchi et al., 2000; Craig, Mullan & Blaxland, 2010). According to the 30 "doing gender" approach (West & Zimmermann, 1987), women and men can perceive the problem of reconciliation between paid work and family responsibilities differently. For men, work activities can be an instrument to exercise their role of "providers" in line with prevalent social norms. For women, as social norms have traditionally ascribed the role of family care giver to them, time spent on paid work outside the family often conflicts with that spent for the family at home. Other theories focus on the role of individual resources in the allocation of time for childcare. According to the theory of "relative resources and bargaining power" (Lundberg & Pollak, 1996; Lunderg & Rose, 1999), the higher the job position and the professional success of an individual, and the higher his/her share of (household) income, the greater is his/her bargaining power within the household with regard to unpaid domestic work (Thomson 1990). Hence, roles are not solely predetermined by gender, but are also strongly influenced by the relative earning power of each partner.

In increasingly prevalent non-traditional family forms, especially stepfamilies, family management is an even more complex issue. The "doing family" approach, which is an extension of the "doing gender" approach, is considered useful when studying such complex family forms (Morgan, 1999; Smart, 2000; Nelson, 2006). Similar to the 'doing gender' approach, the 'doing family' approach stresses that family life is socially constructed. It focuses on how families embed their everyday family lives in internal daily routines such as doing meals and (e.g. bed time) rituals, including activities and time with children, housework, and external social activities such as work as well as unexpected events e.g. illness of a child or frequent business trips (Jurczyk et al., 2009). It is assumed that the organization of family life poses greater challenges for stepfamilies than for traditional nuclear families since their family network (internally and externally) is much more complex. For example, although former partners live separated they may still be linked together in many ways; children whose parents live apart may move between the homes of the parents; (step)grandparents may become essential in creating family, that is managing everyday family life. Thus the increase of non-traditional family constellations calls for a closer exploration of "doing family" in such multi-local family types (Schier & Proske, 2010).

Empirical findings and research gaps

Despite the growing tendency towards blurring boundaries in modern societies, we know fairly little about its consequences for gender roles and gender practices in families, which may interact with changing working conditions. There is some research in the U.S. which looked at certain dimensions of flexibility and their impacts on families (Hochschild, 1997; Presser, 2003). For Europe, the Globalife Project examined the consequences of globalization on the life course of men and women (Mills et al., 2005). Literature on breadwinning women in western societies is rather limited. The few quantitative studies on the topic usually have a national focus (see Eggebeen & Knoester, 2001; Bloemen & Stancanelli, 2007 for France; Kanji, 2013 for the UK; for the US see Brennan, Barnett & Gareis, 2001; Winkler, McBride & Andrews, 2005). Qualitative studies from the US focus mostly on gender-identity in relation to breadwinning women (Macmillan & Gartner, 1999; Medved, 2009; Meisenbach, 2010; Chesley, 2011).

Findings on the relationship between the work status of women and the division of household work are somewhat mixed. Many studies suggest that women still do the bulk of housework regardless their working arrangement (see Grunow et al., 2012; Zabel & Heintz-Martin, 2012; Bianchi et al., 2000). There is no uniform evidence that full-time working women have a more egalitarian division of household duties than part-time working women do (Wengler, Trappe & Schmitt, 2008; Keddi & Zerle-Elsäßer, 2012), nor is there consistent evidence that breadwinning women refuse to follow a traditional role segregation with regard to household tasks (Klenner, Menke & Pfahl, 2012; Klammer, Neukirch & Weßler-Poßberg, 2012). So far, there are still research gaps as to how they deal with the multiple burden of work and household, family life and/or fertility decisions, in particular under conditions of new forms of family life and multi-local families, and how they handle the every-day challenges in practice (Knijn & Smit, 2009; Rijken & Knijn, 2009).

As women are more active in the labor market and are increasingly highly educated, their expectations about fathering and fathers' behavior concerning the reconciliation of work and family are changing. Studies on "new fathers" suggest that young families strive for an equal (or more equal) division of labor (S. Lewis, 1997; Fthenakis, 1999; Bianchi et al., 2000; Zulehner, 2003;

Matzner, 2004; Zerle & Krok 2008; United Nations, 2011). Parental leave uptake by fathers, flexible work practices and how they include care-giving in their construction of masculinity have been studied by Brandth and Kvande (1998, 2001, 2002) and by O'Brien, Brandt and Kvande (2007).

Empirical evidence of how mothers' employment is associated with fathers' time with children is inconclusive (see studies reviewed by Craig, 2007; Pailhé & Solaz, 2008). Similarly, there are mixed findings on the extent to which fathers' own employment schedules are associated with their time with children (Sayer, Bianchi & Robinson, 2004; Romano & Bruzzese, 2007; Pailhé & Solaz, 2008). Conversely, in a recent comparative study Craig and Mullan (2011) find that parent's work arrangements and education relate only modestly to shares of childcare, but this relationship depends on the context. Other European studies find a higher degree of participation in childcare among more educated fathers with more children and with a working partner (Di Giulio & Carrozza, 2003; Smith, 2004; Tanturri, 2006; Tanturri & Mencarini, 2009).

The different theories typically used to explain gender imbalance and negotiations within the couples seem not to be completely adequate to explain the division of childcare between partners (Hofferth, 2001; Bittman, Craig & Folbre, 2004; Craig and Bittman, 2008). Unlike housework, which is reduced as paid work hour increase, mothers maintain their childcare time by cutting back on their own leisure, personal care, and sleep (Craig, 2007). This suggests that employed mothers may actively limit fathers' care through gate-keeping and hampering their involvement with the children. Mothers might do this because they wish to retain control of a domain they feel expert in, or they do not trust fathers to deliver as high a standard of care as they themselves provide (Bianchi & Milkie, 2010; Craig & Mullan, 2011). Father's time with children may reflect parents' different values, resources, and opportunities (Coltrane, 2007). In addition, father's time with children varies across countries according to welfare regimes, family and employment policies and the tax and benefit system, as well as social norms (Gornick & Meyers, 2009; Lewis, 2009; Anxo et al., 2011). Interesting examples of comparative research in European countries can be found in Gauthier, Smeeding & Furstenberg (2004), Sullivan et al. (2009), Anxo et al. (2011), Craig & Mullan (2011), Smith Koslowski (2011); Hook & Wolfe (2012). Yet little research has examined cross-national differences in how childcare is shared between partners within various types of households in different welfare regimes and very few studies have explored in detail which type of childcare fathers perform compared to mothers.

The complexity of everyday family life is even more pronounced in stepfamilies. The division of housework in such families (Snoeckx, Dehertogh & Mortelmans, 2008), their sociodemographic characteristics and their economic well-being are quite well documented (Kreyenfeld & Martin, 2011). However, little research exists on how such families live their lives (Daly, 2003; Rönkä & Pirjo, 2009). The subjective well-being of children in stepfamilies is one indicator of fulfilled family life, because children are also an important part of the construction of the family life and the "success" of stepfamilies could depend on them. McDonald and DeMaris (2002) showed that stepchildren who have a strong relationship with the non-resident biological parent are most likely to have a poor relationship to the stepfather, if he strongly demands conformity. The relationship between the absent father and the child depends on the contact with him and the age of the child at separation (e.g. Weiss, 1982; Ainsworth, 1982; Cherlin & Furstenberg, 1994; Pasley & Moorefield, 2004). Stepfamily research often focuses on child and/or adolescent outcomes such as emotional and behavioral problems (Najman et al., 1997; Dunn et al., 1998; O'Connor et al., 2001) or emotional well-being (Sweeny, 2007).

An overview of empirical literature showed little evidence that children in stepfamilies differ from children in other family types (Ganong & Coleman, 1984; Amato & Keith, 1991; Amato, 1994).

A further important aspect is the relationship between grandparents and grandchildren, which has not been studied broadly until recently (Uhlendorff, 2003). Since people are living to older and older ages, multigenerational bonds are becoming increasingly important (Bengston, 2001). A large body of studies has focused on the frequency of contact and the relationship closeness between grandparents and grandchildren (e.g. Uhlenberg & Hammill, 1998) but not on specific interactions (Mueller et al., 2002). Within the context of stepfamilies grandparents can have a stabilizing role during the separation process (Lussier et al., 2002). In other cases, when a separated partner does not support further contact to the "ex" parents-inlaw, they might even lose contact to their grandchildren (Cherlin & Furstenberg, 1992). Grandparents in turn can also become step-grandparents and the question how they deal with such non-biological relatives might be an important research question. Studying grand parenting in stepfamilies can be very complex as a variety of relationships might be of interest, such as biological grandparenthood versus step-grandparenthood (Hagestad, 2006).

A shocking new study released by the Pew Research Center on May 29, 2013 reported that women were the primary or sole source of income in 40 percent of U.S. households with children under the age of 18. That means they make more than their husbands, or that they are the only ones making money for the household either because their husbands don't work or because they are single moms.

This record-breaking statistic is just one of many brought out in the report that outlines America's rapidly changing demographics. In 1960, seven in ten families with children consisted of a father who was the breadwinner and a wife who was the homemaker. Today, barely three in ten have that setup. Families in America are shifting more and more from what was previously the accepted norm.

The idea of a husband being the primary supporter of the family is no longer the popular belief. Only 28 percent of adults believed it was better for a marriage if the husband earned more money than the wife. This is no surprise: In nearly a quarter of all marriages in the United States, the wife already makes more than her husband.

The report showed that when a married woman made more than her husband, the family income was about $2,000 more than that of families that had the husband as the primary breadwinner, and $10,000 more than that of families where couples made the same amount.

The report also showed that most Americans have no desire to go back to the traditional family: Seventy-nine percent of Americans rejected the idea that women need to return to their traditional roles. The majority of people don't want to go back to the traditional family organization, yet at the same time will agree that this new family pattern isn't making life easier. Though Americans have a less negative assessment of forsaking the traditional family than they did 15 years ago, people are still admitting that life is harder when the wife works outside the home: Seventy-four percent of the people interviewed agreed that it is harder to raise children and 50 percent agreed that it was harder to make a marriage successful.

And yet, even though people admit that life is harder without a mother at home, they don't see it as a major issue. Today, 34 percent of Americans think that a child is just as well off if the mother works. They don't think that a mother's role at home is important. And apparently most mothers agree. The study showed that almost two thirds of mothers with children younger than 6 were either employed or looking for work. However, a lot of these would be single mothers who would have to work out of necessity.
But that of course raises another issue. There is also a growing lack of concern for the need for family at all. Only 64 percent of people think that the growing number of children born to unmarried mothers is a big problem. This is 7 percent less than what it was five years ago. But the trend is even

more troubling when you consider that it is the young people who are least concerned with this problem. Of the people polled ages 18 to 29, only 42 percent thought this was a big problem. The majority in this age category don't see it as a big problem.

For years the Trumpet has been warning of the social upheavals in the world, particularly in America and American families. Few realize the importance of strong, stable, traditional families. In the March 2009 edition of the Trumpet, editor in chief Gerald Flurry wrote, "History shows that the strength of any nation depends on the strength of its families. Family is the rock-solid foundation on which a country's superstructure is erected. That was the case for both America and Britain. ... Today, most people have rejected the law of cause and effect. We think we can discard marriage and family and suffer no consequences ...."

In Isaiah 3, God foretold that in these present latter days, family breakdown and the rise of women leading the family would be the norm. Though it may be generally accepted today, God never intended women to be the chief providers in the family.

That may fly in the face of what many feminists say, but it is the simple truth of the Bible. God created the man to be the primary breadwinner of the home. In fact, God condemns those men who don't provide for their families. The woman was intended to be a help for her husband, keeping the home while he is at work. There is a set pattern in place that God established to preserve unity in a marriage and in a family.

How we need our moms! This is a truth most of us know intuitively, but which nevertheless has been borne out by several studies. Though some would downplay the importance of authoritative parental influence on children, their efforts are undermined by facts.

Consistently, studies have shown that the emotional development of the child—the capacity to love and to form attachments to other human beings—is greatest from conception to age 3. A secure attachment to a parent—which is severely inhibited by day care according to a 1999 National Institute of Child and Human Development study—is "related to the child's development of self-confidence and social competence." Stronger parental attachments lay a sturdy emotional foundation upon which that child can more adequately develop good social skills.

Sadly, more and more children are growing up without that influence. According to one study, between 1965 and the late 1980s, the amount of time children spent interacting with parents dropped 43 percent. A 1992 study conducted at Stanford University, comparing statistics from 1960 and 1986, found that parents were spending 10 to 12 hours less time with children each week.

A big part of the reason for these changes is the exodus of women out of the home and into the workforce. In 1950, 26 percent of married women between the ages of 25 and 44 were employed outside the home. By the early 2000s, that figure grew to about 72 percent; among women with babies under age 1, 58 percent now worked. Also, while men and single women work about the same number of hours as they did 50 years ago, among married women, weekly hours of work outside the home have tripled.

And consider: Among working mothers who believe they "have to" work, more than half admit they would continue working even if they didn't need the money (Andrew Hacker, The Case Against Kids). That's right: Half the working mothers in America freely admit they would rather be at work all day than at home with children.

Anyone who believes that mothers are unimportant in the lives of their children should consider the problems that have resulted from moms leaving home on such a mass scale.

Children left home alone are far likelier to abuse alcohol, tobacco or marijuana, and far more likely to engage in sexual activity. Lack of parental involvement even has a proven negative effect on a child's studies. In a book by Harvard School of Public Health researcher Jody Heymann, an examination of more than 1,600 children revealed that "parental absence between 6 and 9 p.m. was particularly harmful. For every hour a parent worked during that interval, a child was 16 percent more likely to score in the bottom quarter of a standardized math test. The results held true even after taking into account family income, parental education, marital status, the child's gender and the total number of hours the parents worked" (The Widening Gap).

These studies prove that, on the whole, just as surely as plants need water and sunlight, children wither without motherly influence and flourish with it. This is a truth long ago expounded on in a source that too few recognize today as being authoritative: The Bible.

Let's get God's perspective on this all-important subject.

After creating the man, God said, "It is not good that the man should be alone; I will make him a help meet for him." God didn't want the man to be alone—it wasn't good. He knew the man would need help. But why did the man need help? How did God intend for the woman to help man the most?

The Hebrew word for meet means opposite. In the same way men and women are altogether different physically, their roles within the family are profoundly different. Though they are absolutely equal in importance, God meant for both roles to perfectly complement each other, not to compete with one another. Each role enables the other to accomplish much more than either could alone.

How can a wife best support and assist her husband? He admonished the older women in the Church to teach the younger women "good things". He explains—teach the younger ones to love their husbands and to love their children! Verse 5 continues the thought: "To be discreet, chaste, keepers at home, good, obedient to their own husbands, that the word of God be not blasphemed." Love your husband, love your children and keep the home, or "guide the house."

Feminists cringe at the thought. Instead of teaching young girls about it, they ridicule and mock the way God organized the family. They view any attempt to persuade working moms to return home as an attack on women's rights. They would rather compete with men to prove they are every bit as capable of holding a successful career.

And while they have proven that, it has come at considerable cost. Our children have suffered immeasurably.

"The rod and reproof give wisdom: but a child left to himself bring his mother to shame." Generally speaking, of course, a child left to himself brings shame on both parents. But maybe God gets specific in this proverb for a reason.
After all, one of a man's God-given responsibilities requires that he work—usually outside the home. Paul said that if a man won't provide for his family, he is worse than an infidel. And if a mother is to be the "keeper at home" while the husband is away at work, she obviously will spend more time with the children. It doesn't mean the father is without responsibility at home. Not at all! But when he is at work during the day, mom is in charge. And because of the time spent with the children, she is more directly involved in their training and development—especially when they are young. Perhaps this is why God singles out the mother in the proverb.

If a father abdicates his responsibilities as loving head and provider, if he abandons his wife and family, forcing mom to go it alone and to step outside her role as a woman, it brings on him the greatest possible shame.

In like manner, when a mother chooses to abandon her children—leaving them alone—it brings great shame on her.

God never meant for us to be alone, whether father, mother or child. He organized the family so that no one would be left alone, so long as everyone willingly accepted their roles. In the case of mothers, the best way by far they can help their children is to stay at home with them, providing constant care and loving supervision.

The mother's role is not about stifling yourself, your talents, your uniqueness. It's about growing, working, developing yourself—and marshaling all those abilities in building the family, channeling all that energy into serving your husband and your family.

When this role is fulfilled, everyone benefits—husband, wife and children. According to biblical commands, mothers should be highly honored for the tremendous role they play in our families. The Fifth Commandment includes God's command to honor your mother. The Apostle Peter tells husbands to give honor to the wife. This should also be happening within our families today.

ROLES OF MEN IN MARRIAGE

What defines a man in the 21st century? How they are handling new expectations? Is it possible to bring up a healthy generation without a father figure?

The change of manhood. What are these new 21st century requirements?

A few decades ago, men were considered to be providers and protectors; today, a lot of discussions are centered around gender equality, and nowadays women around the world are fighting fiercely to make sure their rights are respected. It may seem that the traditional notion of male is dying out as women today have equal career opportunities, are able to provide for a family, and their interests are not limited to creating a cozy home for their husbands. Even more, the amount of stay-at-home dads has significantly increased as women are pursuing their careers and even military field is available for them these days.

Today, more women are earning higher salaries and can afford to be pickier while choosing a partner, and often ladies are the initiators of divorce. Still, sexism is present in every day acts like cat calling, inappropriate jokes at the office, and many more.

Nowadays, women make up the majority of college and grad school students, while not all men are fans of continuing education and read books in their spare time. Areas in science and technology, traditionally considered to be men's domains, now belong to women. Best universities are open for women, and men should catch up in order not to be left behind. It is vital for men to become better and stronger to prove their ability to remain protectors. Improving own skills, setting and achieving goals, being masculine – this is what expected from men.

Expectations are getting higher, and students should do their best to be successful in universities in order to have better career prospects. This is possible with reliable writing service that provides outstanding academic papers on time, written by expert English speaking writers. Affordable prices, strict adherence to deadlines as well as to any other requirements, complete confidentiality, professional customer support team are what is making this custom writing service the leader on this market. Entrusting expert writers with an essay or thesis will save a lot of time and efforts and allow you to settle some other issues.

Man's role in the family

Up until this century, men's and women's roles were fairly well-defined: woman was expected to be a mother and a wife, taking care of husband's well-being and raising children and man had to provide for his family. Today, the line between male's and female's roles is becoming more blurred as women tend to be as ambitious in business word as men.

Role of a man in a family included the following functions:

• A protector;
• A leader;
• A teacher,

But even this can be handled by women today. So, who is a man today? A hunter and protector or the nurturer, who takes a maternity leave and lives with a bread-winning wife?

Our modern society gives men a chance to be much more connected with their families and women are, finally, getting an opportunity to develop identities that are not defined solely by motherhood. Still, a lot of women prefer a man to play the role of a leader. So, what a modern man should do for self-improvement, to prove that he can be a leader not only in business world but in his own family?

• It will be useful to learn a new language. It can be used in your work or for travelling;
• Read more in order to be interesting to talk to. Watch less TV;
• Start sport training;
• Create a healthy diet;
• Improve your relationship with your wife, family or girlfriend;
• Improve your working performance, aim for promotion;
• Make a budget;
• Try improving your confidence;
• Know how to say "no;"
• Invest in your education, health, and appearance.

Women of 21st century are as strong and capable as men; moreover, they tend to be economically independent, and these basic recommendations will help to improve man's masculinity and enrich individuality.

Importance of a father figure in child's and family's life

Parenting involves two people raising children together, but, nowadays, children in developed countries tend to be growing up in fatherless homes. It is known that children from single-parent families tend to have more difficulties in grown up life and some studies suggest that kids, that were raised without a father and had no father figure in their lives, are more likely to be aggressive and quick to anger, involved in illegal activities, be dropped out of schools and universities due to lack of effort and motivation and having psychological and emotional problems stopping them from creating own families.

On the other hand, children raised by caring fathers have better educational outcomes, better verbal skills, intellectual functioning, and many other advantages. No matter what the current state of manhood is, the role of a husband and a father is invaluable and will never be substituted. Traditional values are worth fighting for and deserve for existence in order to create healthy generations.

Family is an assembly of people who have marital relation and blood related individuals, living under the same roof. A group of many families living together is considered a society. In other words, family is a cell of a modern society. Each and every individual has the responsibility of building up the family in order to create a happy family. In the current world, the man plays a very special role which affects not only his current family but also later generations.

There is a saying in Vietnamese: "Men are the ones who build the house, while women are the one who create the home", we can see that the man is always the strong one, who does the heaviest work for his family, but it does not mean that the man's role is just to support the family in financing, building the house, providing settlement then living all the rest of the family's duties to the woman to do all the household chores such as raising children or house caring, the man and the woman have to share with each other about every aspect of living life and family's side. Being a man of the family is not a simple thing, he has to show all of his strengths to build up his family which seems to be a difficult work for all men in the world.

Marriage is a combination of the man and the woman, according to Mignon McLaughlin, "a successful marriage requires falling in love many times, always with the same person". To become the man of the family, firstly, he has to be a good husband. A good husband is the man who understands his wife's needs and wants. Any woman wants her husband to be a successful man and always willing to share with her all problems in life, like Zig Ziglar (also known as Hilary Hinton Ziglar) said before: "Many marriages would be better if the husband and the wife clearly understood that they are on the same side".

For the Christians, when a man and a woman are getting married, they always promise to love each other forever and be side by side through sickness, poverty, even the hardest times of life, richness or healthy in the church. So, we can easily see that love is the first requirement of being a husband. The husband needs to give his wife the love and regards her like a woman and a person, not a maid for free in the house. Intense love, compassion, altruism, understanding of the husband is the thing woman wants the most. A man who has a warm heart, always opens his mind to listen to his wife is an ideal husband. Listening and understanding is always the important thing to do for his wife because "Shared joy is a double joy, shared sorrow is half a sorrow" said by Swedish Proverb. Woman loves by eyes and ears, thus she will be very happy when she gets a good compliment from the husband. When the wife feels happy, she will do everything to make her family become happier and happier, fully filled with love.

Dividing the responsibilities in a family is different, depend on the culture. For instance, it is common for a Japanese household that the husband is the one who goes to work, giving financial support for the whole family, while the wife usually retreats from her previous work, willingly take care of all the house chores and raising children. Rarely, the husband will do some part of the chores when he feels like to, or under "pressure" from other parties (his spouse, children, etc.). In this situation, the man of the family becomes the main financial provider. In the modern life, other "hard works", such as fixing or maintaining the house's equipment can be done by paying to a third party service, thus making money becomes the most important assignment that the man has to concentrate on.

Aside from that, the man in the house must also have well personality, good insight and knowledgeable. Moreover, contributing to the emotional, spiritual, physical and mental well-being of his family are all necessary. In order to do this, he must recognize that there are other elements other than money are needed to be provided. The man mainly takes this part in family's duties.

When the need of love and financial are fulfilled, the woman will need a strong man to protect her family. That is an important duty of the husband. Not only protecting the family, the man should also be the first one to solve all the problems. That does not mean that the husband is the only one who has to do all the problem-solving part, but that he should do it instead of waiting for his partner to ask for help or push him up. A role-model husband is not the one who knows everything or does everything, but the one who has the ability to balance every duty, giving it the most suitable priority.

Nowadays, there are many women choose to be single mothers. They are confident that even when lacking the support of the men, they can still be able to live well, raising the children to become good people without the need of their children's father. However, that will not give the children all the care they need, as a proverb in Vietnamese: "the child without his/her father is similar to the house without its roof".

On the other hand, the mother cannot teach her child all the skills that the child's father can do. No matter how masculine the woman is, there are always tasks that only men can do. Become a mother is a proof of how the feminine she is already. How can she raise her son to become a real man, without the affection of all the feminine she has? And how can she give her precious girl a good imagine of the daughter's future partner? They will just simply take all the trait of their only parent, thus hardening all the tasks on the mother, will may not relevant at early age, but become more clearly as they grow up.

Furthermore, children are always longed more love and care, and will easily get jealous if they see that they are not getting as much attention as other kids. Whenever they see other children's fathers sending them to school, or playing sport together, immediately there will be countless questions arise in the lonely child mind: "Do I have a father? Who is my father? Why had he never appeared in my life?" As the consequence, all that questions will be turned to the mother, which will surely be in an uncomfortable situation when being asked like that. At that time, is there any explanation that understand able to the children without hurting them, or will other lies be given that put the children in deeper confusion?

A life without a man in the family will cause many difficulties to the woman. For now, she will have to do all the house works, while taking care of the kids and keeping the family's financial situation at an acceptable rate. How does she suppose doing all that jobs at the same time? If the woman is in a rich family, or she already has a well-paying job, then the tasks can be less pressuring. However, those are only rare exceptions. On the contradict, many single mothers having trouble balancing the duties all at once. Hence, she will need a man to share all the weight on her shoulder, in order to keep the family happy and affluent at all time. Taking care of the children must not come from the thought that is it the duty as the parents, but from the immeasurable and unconditional love to their blood related children.

Educating the kids is not an individual task. It must be done by both the parents, taken will well care and be treasured. Children are especially sensitive, and always eager to learn new things from the world. Every little thing from the outer environment will affect their perspective, which decides the children's behavior when they grow up. They will just simply mimic all what they think that are interesting. The worst thing is, the actions that the children try to mimic may not be all right. Supposedly there may be bad behaviors such as bullying or pick pocketing. As time goes by, they will consider that those actions are the righteous, without regarding its true meaning. Therefore, as the nearest source of affection the children, parents always have to act as role model, not only while teaching their kid, but in everyday actions. Similar to growing a tree, if well-tended had not been taken since it was a seed, the tree might not give out its expected juicy fruit.

For example, considering a family of the sporty type, in which there are many sports activities are done by both the father and the son. The boy will soon get the habit of doing sport, and keep practicing them when he grows up. Soon enough, that man will spread his hobby to the next generation, when he starts having family on his own. In the family of the arguing type, where parents always shout at each other for every trivial, the children will pick up that pattern, and become ill-mannered in no time. That cycle will continue forever, until there are changes in the new family.

However, that does not mean that any successful man will also success in being a father. Sometime, the man's mind sways away with his busy career, thus forgetting his duty as a father, neglecting his responsibility of teaching the kids. Only when he is at the top of the career ladder, and his children have already on the completely wrong track, he will realize his own carelessness. Therefore, it is necessary for the man to balance between the family and the job.

For a girl, the father is usually taken as the model for her boyfriend or future life partner. If the relationship between father and daughter is close and they often have conservations together, the girl will be more confident in choosing boyfriend, better understanding of the opposite gender, thus avoid misunderstandings and unnecessary worries. As a female, when the girl gets dressed, she wants to be the center of the attentions, so if the father can understand and commend on her dresses, it will affect to her way of dressing and living and then leading to a familiar life suitable to her family and society. A boy always has his secret which is not easy to say out and he is easy to be influent by his friends' bad habits, if he has a good guider who encourage his mind and knowledge, he will be prevented from the wrong way in his life. And the boy is deeply getting his father character's effect. If a boy grows up without a father, he cannot get along well with all the boy's problems, mother cannot share all the secrets with her son. Boys are more difficult and they often act like his father does.

In conclusion, the man in the family plays a very important role in the family. He has to perform the duty of not only the husband, the father but also the mental leader. As a husband, he has to understands and sympathizes with his wife, his soul-mate. As a father, he has the responsibility to teach his son and daughter the skills needed to become good people. As a mental leader, he has to remain calm and strong in any situations. It is not easy to perform all those tasks perfectly simultaneously, but with a strong heart and a clear determination, nothing is impossible.

Once upon a time, men and women went into marriage with very clear ideas about their duties and responsibilities. The husband went out to work while the wife remained home and cooked, cleaned and brought up the children. The responsibility of the traditional wife was to make the home a place of order, peace, and tranquility: whereas the husband came back in the evening to rejuvenate himself. However, the reality of 2018 is entirely different.

The Roles of a Modern Husband

Statistics tell it all

In 2015, <u>38% of wives</u> earned more than their husbands.

<u>70% of working mothers</u> are full-time employees.

These realities mean that the responsibilities around the home have had to be revised: the husband is no longer the primary breadwinner and it is no longer realistic for the wife to do it all at home by herself.

New realities

And it is not only in the job market that things have changed. For instance, the traditional man was also a handyman. In contrast, the modern man has no idea what goes on in his boiler and probably can't reliably fix the toilet. The modern husband is increasingly relying on professionals for home repairs, an interchange that can sting with emasculation.

Changes in the last few decades have redefined the responsibilities and roles of husbands.

There is no longer the romantic notion that was attached to 'providing' and undertaking 'masculine jobs.'

As a result, many husbands have become confused and insecure. They do not know how to act at home, and, consequently, they have become passive. Some husbands have decided that the easiest thing to do is nothing. With both feet planted firmly in mid-air, they have allowed the wife to take over. How does a husband remain relevant when the things that defined him a few years ago are no longer strictly his forte?

The 21st century husband and the house chores

The reality of 2018 is that only a handful of working parents have 'the village' that they need to care for their children. The 2018 woman cannot completely replicate herself while she is at work: She may pay for childcare and even a cleaning service, but that is still not enough. Therefore, husbands have had to come in to relieve their wives at home. It is no longer enough for the 2018 husband to just 'man' the grill for the occasional BBQ.

The 2018 husband cannot claim to love his wife and then watch while she toils at home after a long day at work. Even if she is a stay at home mum, there is a new understanding that housework is every bit as exhausting as going out to earn an income, if not more. Loving your wife means recognizing that she is exhausted and overwhelmed. If you love your wife, and you want her to feel loved, you will get home and slide into the second part of your day's schedule, just like her.

Co-inherence

According to Charles William, true intimacy in a relationship comes when you and your wife can identify so closely with each other that you see yourselves in each other: co-inherence. When you master co-inherence, you will not grumble about helping your wife with household chores.

Always remind yourself that your wife is your best friend and there are many little things you can do to make things easier for her:

Ask your wife to draw up a list of the invisible tasks.

Be attentive about the work that needs to be done every day and do some of it.

Recognize the effort and sacrifice involved in completing the remainder of the work.

Remember, the point is not really to do only half the work. It is helping your wife as much as you can. The motto should be: nobody sits until everybody sits. If there is work to be done and your wife is up, you are up too, doing what needs to be done.

Fatherhood in 21st century

The modern father greatly differs from the traditional married income earner and disciplinarian. He comes in various forms: employed or stay at home, biological, adoptive or stepparent. He is more than capable of being a caregiver for his children for both their physical and psychological challenges.

Research by National Institute of Child Health and Human Development revealed that fathers who are more involved in caregiving:

Have positive psychological adjustment effects on their children (lower levels of hostility and depression; higher self-esteem and coping with adulthood).

Improve their children's cognitive development and functioning.

Report greater intimacy with their wives.

Further, the study showed that the role of a father's love in his children's development is great as the influence of the mother's love. Therefore, maintaining a healthy relationship with your wife contributes significantly to your children's health and wellbeing.

The husband must work closely with his wife to provide emotional and financial support for the children, provide appropriate monitoring and discipline and most importantly, remain a permanent and loving presence in both his wife's and his children's lives.

The modern husband and provision

Most people believe that being a good provider means supporting one's family financially. This is the reason many husbands are left insecure and confused when their wives start earning an income as well; sometimes even more than theirs.

Provision means much more than finances. A husband must also provide the emotional, physical, mental and spiritual well-being of his family.

As a husband, the biggest realization that you can come to is that, in addition to money, there are other currencies that you are called upon to provide in your family.

The modern husband and protection

Protecting your family means more than being the master of your household's alarm system, being in charge of opening the door when someone knocks at night and shutting the household down before bed. It is beyond beating up the guy next door if he insults your wife.

You need to have your wife's back, even if it means protecting her from your own family.

Heck, you may even have to protect your wife from your own children! Show others that you will not tolerate any disrespect towards your wife.

Protection also extends to taking care of your wife's emotional needs.

Beware how you speak to your wife. Like dropping a delicate piece of China, your words can break your wife permanently.

In addition, protect your wife's self-esteem. Nobody else can make your wife feel like a supermodel despite the sagging breasts and stretch marks.

The modern husband and leadership

Part of being a husband is responsibility. It is realizing that you are no longer alone. You have a team that needs to be guided and protected from disunity. Effective marriages, like effective teams, need to be led with a servant leader attitude.

Contrary to popular belief, women do not want to wear pants in the family.

Evidence indicates that despite the strides that women have made economically, most do not want to be their families' leaders. Many wives want their husbands to lead. And what's more, men don't want to be led by their wives.

So, do not wait for your wife to take the initiative when there are problems in your family. Take the lead. Get in the game and create the kind of a family you want instead of wasting time whining about your family's situation.

Remember, you will get the family you create, not the one you think you deserve.

What about sex?

Traditionally, there were clear-cut attitudes about intimacy; the man's wishes were what counted. You do not believe that anymore, neither does your wife. However, there is still the expectation that a husband should take leadership in a couple's sexual lives.

You must realize that your wife is probably still inhibited by the traditional attitudes.

Always seek to add new adventures to take your sex lives to the next level. Remember, the level of satisfaction with your sex life will determine the level of satisfaction in your marriage.

Husbands must adapt to the realities of modern time

Research shows that husbands are happier when their wives are homemakers. It seems that many husbands are still operating using the chauvinistic social codes that were established during the last century. Unfortunately, this is only hurting families. You must learn to be adaptive to the present day realities in order to build a healthy marriage.

Communication

At the heart of marriage problems, today is unclear expectations and contradictory goals. Shared expectations and mutual understanding of each partner's primary goals and roles will save your marriage from dissatisfaction, arguing and misunderstandings. Today's couples require communication skills to run a successful relationship. This is where your leadership comes in.

Find a way for you and your wife to communicate your needs and responsibilities openly and clearly with each other.

Create an environment where you talk about everything. You will establish a fulfilling relationship on a scale that you have never imagined.

Lastly, don't feel threatened

Do not be threatened because your wife has a job or that she is out-earning you. Men and women are not the same; thus, they are not interchangeable. Even if you and your wife are capable of doing what each other can do, it does not mean that you are both capable of performing all tasks with equal fervor. And, it doesn't even mean you will both be happy if you do. With constant communication with your wife, you will always find equilibrium in your relationship.

WHEN ONE PERSON CONTROLS THE RELATIONSHIP

It would be nice if every relationship had a straight 50/50 power dynamic split…but those in relationships will tell you that's probably not the case in their partnership. Relationships *should* be about a shared, equal bond, where partners are teammates who make compromises and share power, rather than a coach versus team member dynamic. Right?

Think about this common question couples get asked: "So, who wears the pants in this relationship?" Usually, pop culture tells us the man in a heterosexual couple should "wear the pants." If the woman "wears the pants" the man is looked at as "whipped" and sometimes even teased for it. By talking about and asking who's *wearing the pants*, we're perpetuating the idea that one person should be in charge.

It's like society *demands* one person hold more power in the relationship. What happened to equality?

Why Dominant Roles Exist in Relationships

There are multiple reasons why one person may exert more power in a relationship.

"[Roles in relationships] depend on experiences in our lives," Kimberly Leitch, LCSW-R and Talk-space therapist, says, "Someone may have been in a controlling relationship previously and now they tend to be in control of their present relationship in fear of repeating the same mistakes. The importance of balance varies with each person."

Of course, there are other life events that can cause someone to be the controlling partner in a relationship — even events from childhood. For example, if somebody had very controlling parents, it's common that they too might desire control, even in a romantic relationship. Or, if someone experienced lots of rejection as they were growing up, they might take extreme measures in relationships to make sure they aren't rejected or abandoned again.

When it's Okay to Defer to Your Partner

In certain cases, taking ownership of the power dynamic is okay, if it's in a healthy way, and makes sense for each partner.

"There are some personality types that like to relinquish the control onto their partner because they cannot handle the stress of the responsibilities or being in control elicits anxiety." Leitch says. "I have a client whose husband works and therefore she is in charge of everything else [at home] and it works in their relationship. He also tends to be a passive person whereas she is a big personality and tends to be more assertive. He follows her lead and he doesn't have to be bothered making decisions."

In this case, the skewed power dynamic makes sense, so long as the passive partner continues to feel okay with the arrangement, and speaks up if they want more say in decisions around the house.

Even in situations like the one Leitch described, an imbalance of power can definitely turn unhealthy.

"It becomes an issue when you feel like you are not being heard and there is no sense of *you* in the relationship. It can lead you to feel uncomfortable and insecure." Leitch explains, "You may feel like you are submitting to your partner's likes or interests, which is not being reciprocated. It is important to communicate these feelings with your partner to avoid any negative feelings or behaviors."

If you land in a place like this, where you feel like you don't have a voice in your relationship, it's definitely time to reevaluate your partnership and roles. Allowing an unhealthy power dynamic to persist can take a toll on even the strongest relationship.

What to Do When You've Lost Control in a Relationship

Here are some things you can do if you feel like your partner is being too controlling, or the power dynamic has shifted in an unfavorable way.

Be introspective

Look inside yourself and ask *why* you're putting up with being bossed around. Do you feel worthy of healthy love? Are you scared of losing your partner? Are you feeling stuck because you're scared your partner might physically hurt you if you try to leave? Are controlling relationships all you know?

Communicate with your partner

It's possible your partner might not even realize how controlling they're being. Speak up about your feelings, and explain the situation from your point of view in a non-confrontational manner. Spell out scenarios where your partner made you feel poorly about yourself or controlled.

Try to stay calm and level headed. As with any conflict in a relationship, communication is key. While it can be awkward to start a difficult conversation with a partner, learning to do so is crucial.

Be confident and stand strong

All too often, people lose themselves when they are in a controlling relationship. Stand your ground and try to take back some of your power in subtle ways by remaining confident and aware. It may also help to be more independent than usual, which helps you prove to yourself that you can be independent and take care of yourself. Keep your guard up so you can't be so easily manipulated.

Give couples therapy a try

Couples therapy is great for couples who are struggling with any problem. A couple's therapist can provide a safe space for each person to voice their concerns, and the therapist can help facilitate the conversation as well as help the couple understand each other. It can also help ease your nerves if you're scared of confronting your partner one on one.

Recognize signs of abuse

Sadly, domestic abuse is common. Controlling behavior can sometimes be a sign or predictor of abusive behavior. Educate yourself on the signs of domestic abuse so you can be aware of what's going on in your relationship and if things are on the road to getting dangerous.

If you believe you are being abused, tell a loved one and get in touch with an organization like The National Domestic Abuse Hotline for help. This step also goes along with knowing when it's time to walk away from the relationship and leave before it gets any worse.

No Relationship is Perfect, but it Should Be Healthy

While no relationship is perfect, and you shouldn't necessarily strive for "perfect," everybody deserves a safe, healthy relationship. A super controlling partner definitely does not equate to a healthy and happy relationship.

It's okay to share duties and give up control of some areas or aspects of a relationship, but always be aware of your feelings, recognize controlling partners, and look out for the signs of abuse. Nobody deserves to feel powerless or unsafe in a relationship.

MARRIAGE PROBLEMS – RESCUE PLAN

What transitions couples from desperation about their difficulties to delight in sharing their lives together? Here's the 8-step pathway along which are guided to therapy clients—and which you are welcome to take as well.

1. Make a list of all the issues about which you have disagreements.

This includes the issues that you refrain from talking about out of fear that talking might lead to arguing. Your self-help treatment will be complete when you have both found mutually agreeable solutions to all of these issues and have learned the skills to resolve new issues as they arise with similarly win-win solutions.

If the list seems interminable because you fight about everything—from where you should live to the time of day—odds are, the problem is less that you are facing some extraordinarily challenging differences; rather, it's more likely that your manner of talking with each other needs a major upgrade.

2. Fix your focus solidly on yourself.

Attempts to get your partner to change invite defensiveness. No one likes being told they're doing things wrong—or, far worse, that they are a bad person. It's better by far for both of you to each use your energies and intelligence to figure out what YOU could do differently.

Here's a question that can get you started: What would enable you to stay loving and good-humored *even if* the frustrating pieces in your spouse's repertoire never get an upgrade? That's how to become "self-centered" in the best sense. If both of you are seeking to facilitate your own upgrades, the marriage will blossom.

3. Cut the crap.

Pardon my language. But the point is that negative muck that you give each other is totally unhelpful. It only taints a positive relationship. That means no more criticism, complaints, blame, accusations, anger, sarcasm, mean digs, snide remarks...get it?

No more anger escalations either. Stay in the calm zone. Exit early and often if either of you is beginning to get heated. Learn to calm yourself, then re-engage cooperatively.

Research psychologist John Gottman has found that marriages generally survive if the ratio of good to bad interactions is 5 to 1. Do you want to barely survive? Or do you want to save the marriage in a way that will make it thrive? If thriving is your goal, aim for 100,000,000:1. That means: don't sling mud at all. Cut the crap.

4. Learn how to express concerns constructively.

A simple way to do that in sensitive conversations is to stick with the following sentence-starter options. In my clinical work, I give couples a handout that includes these starter phrases. I encourage them to use the handout frequently, checking how to start each comment that might be sensitive or on topics that they know could be prickly. Please feel free to download the full 6-sentence-starters guide; click here and scroll down.

I feel... [followed by a one-word feeling such as "anxious," "sad," etc.]
My concern is...
I would like to... [note: NEVER use "I would like *you* to..."]
How would you feel about that? or *What are your thoughts on that?*

5. Learn how to make decisions cooperatively.

I call collaborative decision-making the "win-win waltz." Win-win decision-making aims for a plan of action that pleases you both. No more insistence designed to "get your way." Instead, when you have differences, quietly express your underlying concerns, listen calmly to understand your partner's concerns, and then create a solution that's responsive to both of your concerns.

Practice this skillset on all the issues you listed in step 1. You may be amazed to discover that, even on issues that seemed intractable, you will be able to co-create solutions that will work for both of you.

6. Eliminate the three A's **that ruin marriages.**

Affairs, Addictions, and excessive Anger are deal-breakers. They are out-of-bounds in a healthy marriage. Fix the habit—or it's game over.

If you or your spouse has these problems, saving this kind of marriage could be a mistaken goal. Better to end a marriage than to continue a marriage with these hurtful habits. Better yet is for each of you to figure out what you can do differently in the future. The one with the A-habit needs to figure out how to end it. The partner needs to heal, and also to learn alternatives to tolerating the habit.

Most importantly, especially if you have children who need you to learn how to be more emotionally healthy as individuals and as a couple, is for the two of you both to commit to building a new kind of marriage.

That is, end the old marriage. Build a new one with the same partner. Build a marriage where there are zero affairs, addictions, or excessive anger and instead, abounding love and trust.

7. Radically increase the positive energies **you give your partner.**

Smile more. Touch more. Hug more. More "eye kisses." More sex. More shared time and shared projects. More appreciation. More dwelling on what you like about your partner.

Respond more often with agreement in response to things your partner says that in the past you might have answered with, "But..." Listening is loving—especially when you are listening to take in information, not to show what's wrong with what your partner says or to show that you know more.

Help out more. Give more praise and more gratitude. Do more fun activities together. Laugh and joke more, do new things, and go new places together. The best things in life really are free. And the more positives you give, the more you'll get. I wrote above about Gottman's 5:1 ratio. Increasing the positives is every bit as important as decreasing negatives to hit a 100,000,000:1 ratio.

8. Look back at your parents' marriage and assess its strengths and weaknesses. Decide what you want to do differently.

When people marry, they bring along a recording in their head of how their parents treated each other, as well as how they were treated by their parents. These relationships are where folks learn patterns of interacting for intimate relationships. Decide consciously what to keep from your folks and what to do differently.

ROMANTIC QUOTES

Though there are many different kinds of love, the romantic love we feel with "the one" – whether we aren't married yet, newlywed, or have been married for decades – is what sets this relationship apart.

Romance – defined as "a feeling of excitement and mystery associated with love" – has inspired writers, poets, musicians, and many others for generations. From the poetry of the Ancient Romans and Greeks to modern day movies, our fascination with love is part of what makes us human.

Keeping the flame of romantic love alive is one of the great challenges of marriage. Work, everyday tasks, pets, household chores, and looking after the kids are just some of the things that can make it difficult to prioritize making time for romance. But Psychology Today warns us that being romantic is a crucial part of maintaining, and growing, your relationship. What's more, couples who fail to find time to be romantic with one another are less likely to stay together than those who do.

Finding romance doesn't have to be difficult or time consuming. It could just be something as simple as turning your phones off during the evening, making time for a coffee date at the weekend, preparing a special meal together, sharing a bath, or kissing one another before leaving the house.

Making your relationship a priority – even when you have a lot on your plate – is vital for a long and happy marriage.

Whether you're looking to remind yourself of the importance of romance, or for a sweet and meaningful way to confess your love to your spouse, these are some of the most romantic quotes ever.

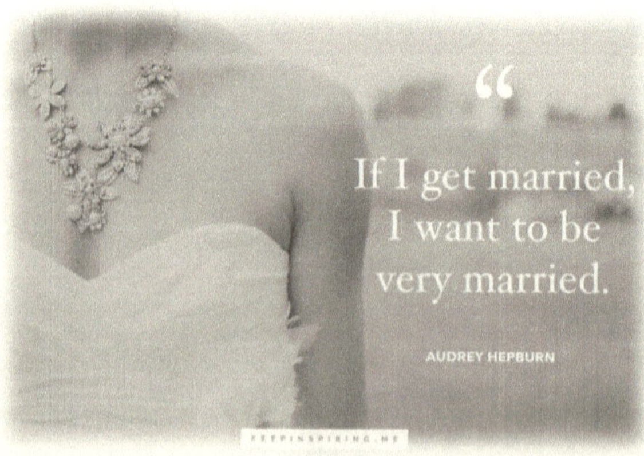

"If I get married, I want to be very married." – Audrey Hepburn

"Let there be spaces in your togetherness, and let the winds of the heavens dance between you. Love one another but make not a bond of love: Let it rather be a moving sea between the shores of your souls. Fill each other's cup but drink not from one cup. Give one another of your bread but eat not from the same loaf. Sing and dance together and be joyous, but let each one of you be alone, even as the strings of a lute are alone though they quiver with the same music. Give your hearts, but not into each other's keeping. For only the hand of Life can contain your hearts. And stand together, yet not too near together: For the pillars of the temple stand apart, And the oak tree and the cypress grow not in each other's shadow."– **Khalil Gibran**, *The Prophet*

"So it's not going to be easy. It's going to be really hard; we are going to have to work every day, but I want to do that because I want you. I want all of you, forever, every day. You and me… every day."– **Nicholas Sparks**

"If I know what love is, it is because of you."– **Hermann Hasse**

"The essence of marriage is companionship, and the woman you face across the coffee urn every morning for ninety-nine years must be both able to appreciate your jokes and to sympathize with your aspirations."– **Elbert Hubbard**

"To be fully seen by somebody, then, and be loved anyhow–this is a human offering that can border on miraculous."– **Elizabeth Gilbert**

"The best love is the kind that awakens the soul and makes us reach for more, that plants a fire in our hearts and brings peace to our minds." – Noah Calhoun

"Love is like a beautiful flower which I may not touch, but whose fragrance makes the garden a place of delight just the same."– **Helen Keller**

"To say that one waits a lifetime for his soulmate to come around is a paradox. People eventually get sick of waiting, take a chance on someone, and by the art of commitment become soulmates, which takes a lifetime to perfect."– **Criss Jami**

"They slipped briskly into an intimacy from which they never recovered."–
F. Scott Fitzgerald

"There is no greater happiness for a man than approaching a door at the end of a day knowing someone on the other side of that door is waiting for the sound of his footsteps."– **Ronald Reagan**

"If I had a flower for every time thought of you… I could walk through my garden forever."– **Alfred Tennyson**

"Every heart sings a song, incomplete, until another heart whispers back. Those who wish to sing always find a song. At the touch of a lover, everyone becomes a poet." – Plato

"I love you without knowing how, or when, or from where. I love you simply, without problems or pride: I love you in this way because I do not know any other way of loving but this, in which there is no I or you, so intimate that your hand upon my chest is my hand, so intimate then when I fall asleep your eyes close."– **Pablo Neruda**

"I'm selfish, impatient and a little insecure. I make mistakes, I am out of control and at times hard to handle. But if you can't handle me at my worst, then you sure as hell don't deserve me at my best."– **Marilyn Monroe**

"What is Love? I have met in the streets a very poor young man who was in love. His hat was old, his coat worn, the water passed through his shoes and the stars through his soul."– **Victor Hugo**

"I am nothing special, of this I am sure. I am a common man with common thoughts and I've led a common life. There are no monuments dedicated to me and my name will soon be forgotten, but I've loved another with all my heart and soul, and to me, this has always been enough."– **Nicholas Sparks**

"Who, being loved, is poor?"– **Oscar Wilde**

"We loved with a love that was more than love." – Edgar Allan Poe

"There is no remedy for love but to love more."– **Henry David Thoreau**

"What greater thing is there for two human souls, than to feel that they are joined for life–to strength each other in all labor, to rest on each other in all sorrow, to minister to each other in silent unspeakable memories at the moment of the last parting?"– **George Eliot**

"There is never a time or place for true love. It happens accidentally, in a heartbeat, in a single flashing, throbbing moment."– **Sarah Dessen**

"You know you're in love when you can't fall asleep because reality is finally better than your dreams."– **Dr. Seuss**

"Your absence has not taught me to be alone, it merely has shown that when together we cast a single shadow on the wall."– **Doug Fetherling**

"When I saw you I fell in love, and you smiled because you knew." – Arrigo Boito

"Marriages are like fingerprints; each one is different and each one is beautiful."**– Maggie Reyes**

"A happy marriage is a long conversation which always seems too short."**– Andre Maurois**

"There are a hundred paths through the world that are easier than loving. But who wants easier?"**– Mary Oliver**

"You don't love someone for their looks, or their clothes, or for their fancy car, but because they sing a song only you can hear."**– Oscar Wilde**

"When you realize you want to spend the rest of your life with somebody, you want the rest of your life to start as soon as possible." –***When Harry Met Sally***

THE SUSTAINABLE MARRIAGE QUIZ

Studies show that the more self-expansion a person experiences through their partner, the more satisfied and committed they are to the relationship. How much is your relationship expanding your knowledge and making you feel good about yourself?

Instructions: Answer each of the 10 questions below according to the way you feel, to see how your own relationship ranks. Take your time and answer truthfully for the most accurate results.

1. How much does being with your partner result in your having new experiences?

- Not very much
- A little
- Somewhat / mixed feeling
- A lot
- Very much

2. When you are with your partner, do you feel a greater awareness of things because of him or her?

- Not very much
- A little
- Somewhat / mixed feeling
- A lot
- Very much

3. How much does your partner increase your ability to accomplish new things?

- Not very much
- A little
- Somewhat / mixed feeling
- A lot
- Very much

4. How much does your partner help to expand your sense of the kind of person you are?

- Not very much
- A little
- Somewhat / mixed feeling
- A lot
- Very much

5. How much do you see your partner as a way to expand your own capabilities?

- Not very much
- A little
- Somewhat / mixed feeling
- A lot
- Very much

6. How much do your partner's strengths as a person (skills, abilities, etc.) compensate for some of your own weaknesses as a person?

- Not very much
- A little
- Somewhat / mixed feeling
- A lot
- Very much

7. How much do you feel that you have a larger perspective on things because of your partner?

- Not very much
- A little
- Somewhat / mixed feeling

○ A lot

○ Very much

8. How much have you learnt new things since you were beside your partner?

○ Not very much

○ A little

○ Somewhat / mixed feeling

○ A lot

○ Very much

9. How much has knowing your partner made you a better person?

○ Not very much

○ A little

○ Somewhat / mixed feeling

○ A lot

○ Very much

10. How much does your partner increase your knowledge?

○ Not very much

○ A little

○ Somewhat / mixed feeling

○ A lot

○ Very much

ABOUT THE AUTHOR

David Bobker is a prolific author who has published over 30 books under several pen names. His purpose as an author is to enlighten and help people through his books.

Previously David has been an Advisory Director at Argyle, Senior Vice President of AST Phoenix Advisors, Managing Director with Georgeson and was one of the founders of Laurel Hill Advisors.

A 1993 graduate of the City University of New York's Brooklyn College with a Bachelor's degree in Computer Science, David earned his MBA in Marketing and Finance from the City University of New York's Baruch College in 2000. David lives with his wife Shoshana, a certified nutritionist, and their seven children in Passaic, New Jersey.